Power

Ethical debates about resources and the environment

KATE RAVILIOUS

Contents

Introduction

Humans are pushing the boundaries of science and technology. We can access information at the touch of a button. We can genetically modify food so that it grows faster and tastes better. We have developed medicines that can cure once-fatal illnesses. All this might sound positive, but we are now facing many dilemmas in the areas of science, technology and medicine. Just because we *can* do something, does this mean we *should*?

Many of these debates are based on what is ethically or morally right – for humans, for animals or for the environment. People often feel very strongly about such issues, whether they are governments, pressure groups or individuals. It is important for everyone to understand what these ethical questions are, and to consider the ways in which they might be solved.

What are natural resources?

How we use the Earth's natural resources is one of the most controversial points of debate in the twenty-first century. So why are they so important, and how has their use come into question?

Wind, water, trees, sunshine, coal, oil, gas, minerals and gemstones – these are just some of the natural resources provided by the planet we live on and

One of the first uses of natural resources was when human ancestors learned to rub sticks together to make fire.

our Solar System. All living things rely on resources; certainly most animals could not survive without water, plants, sunshine and fresh air. Humans depend on these resources more than any other creature.

It all started thousands of years ago when humans first discovered fire. They gradually learned to use resources to help control their environment and become a successful species. Somewhere between 5,000 and 10,000 years ago people began to grow crops, which enabled them to settle in one place. Most of these early people managed to live in balance with the Earth – replenishing the resources as they were used up, or moving on when they ran out.

By the early nineteenth century the Industrial Revolution was in full swing. Steam power (fuelled by coal), machinery, railways, roads and canals transformed the way people lived, leading to mass production of goods and an improved standard of living for many. Suddenly humans started to use up resources at a tremendous pace. Entire forests were cut down, coal seams were mined, hillsides quarried and gallons of water flushed down the drain. This rapid consumption has continued to the present day.

The Industrial Revolution of the nineteenth century resulted in natural resources like coal being used at a much greater rate than ever before. The steam traction engine, used in farming, was one of many technological developments from this period.

Globalisation

Within the last few decades technologies like the telephone, air travel and the Internet have led to globalisation. Our warm homes, fully stocked supermarkets and satellite television all rely on a global chain of resources. One break in that chain, such as a power cut or fuel shortage, can lead to severe disruption. We all depend on resources and the distribution network that moves them around the world.

Today, some natural resources are growing scarce. If we do not plan ahead then we could suffer a collapse in civilisation. There is now a pressing need for everyone to look at the way they live, decide who these resources belong to, how best to use them and how they should be shared out.

1 Environmental Ethics

Not everyone shares the same views about how the environment should be treated and its resources shared. This has led to the formation of a number of organisations, which represent different viewpoints and fight for the causes they believe in.

In 1962 Rachel Carson, an American zoologist and marine biologist, published a book called *Silent Spring*, which highlighted the dangers of pesticides and the threat they pose to wildlife, in particular birds. The book was highly controversial at the time, but it alerted people to the fragility of the Earth's environment and the damage that modern living can inflict.

Pressure groups

By the late 1960s and early 1970s a number of environmental groups had been formed, campaigning for sustainable management of resources and care for the Earth's environment. Some of those groups, like the international organisations Greenpeace and Earth Day Network, are still active today. They organise campaigns and protests, and carry out research to find new solutions.

The groups vary in how confrontational their actions are. Greenpeace uses direct action, with members doing things like chaining themselves to trees to stop them being cut down, or using the Greenpeace ship *Rainbow Warrior* to get in the way of whaling boats. Friends of the Earth (UK) and Earth Day Network usually take a less direct approach and try to get their message across with street protests and educational events. These actions are different ways of expressing opinions about the ethical issues surrounding resources and the environment.

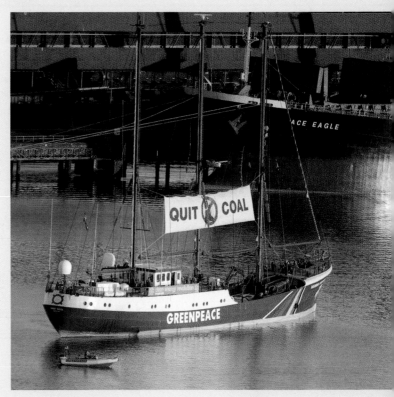

The Greenpeace ship Rainbow Warrior *blocks a coal ship in the Australian port of Newcastle. Groups like Greenpeace take disruptive action in their campaigns against the use of Earth's resources.*

Scientist James Lovelock, whose Gaia hypothesis was one of the earliest suggestions that humans were interfering with the natural balance of the environment.

Gaia theory

Prominent scientists can also influence the way people think about ethical issues. James Lovelock, a British scientist, is famous for the Gaia hypothesis. This is the idea that the Earth behaves as if it were a living organism, where factors like the saltiness of the sea, the amount of oxygen in the air and the cloudiness of the sky are all interacting processes. He has proposed that these processes regulate each other and keep everything in balance. Humans have damaged this balance by overusing resources and filling the atmosphere with greenhouse gases. Lovelock suggests this imbalance is like a disease affecting Gaia, which has brought the Earth to the brink of a crisis.

> ❝ **When the last tree is cut, the last river poisoned, and the last fish dead, we will discover that we can't eat money…** ❞
>
> *Greenpeace banner*

YOU DECIDE

In September 2006 Greenpeace activists chained themselves to a pier at Map Ta Phut in Thailand and delayed the unloading of a shipment of Australian coal for a new power station in Thailand.

? *The activists argued that the power plant will cause climate change, and that Thailand will become reliant on Australian coal instead of investing in renewable energy projects. Are these valid reasons for their actions?*

? *Should people be allowed to demonstrate their feelings in such a direct and disruptive way?*

? *Is direct action like this the best way to get a message across, or can less direct action, like a march along a street, be equally effective?*

Taking action

Not everyone agrees with Gaia theory, but it has revolutionised the way people look at the environment and the effect their own actions can have. Some businesses are responding to public concerns and trying to be more responsible about the way they use the Earth's resources.

In September 2006, billionaire British businessman Sir Richard Branson announced that he would use all the profits from his Virgin air and railway businesses to fight global warming. Around $3 billion over the next 10 years will be invested in a new business venture, Virgin Fuels, which will research more environmentally friendly fuels.

Meanwhile, some politicians and policy-makers are forcing people to change their ways. In the European Union, countries such as Denmark and Germany tax people according to what they throw away. Waste that can be recycled is removed free of charge, but every kilogram of rubbish that needs to go to landfill or incineration must be paid for.

Critics of Richard Branson's Virgin Fuels venture point out that technology will have to advance dramatically before planes can fly on biofuel. They also say that such investment discourages individuals from changing their own behaviour and makes them think they can rely on science to solve the problem.

Many European countries, including Germany, insist on the recycling of household waste, making individuals play a part in helping the environment.

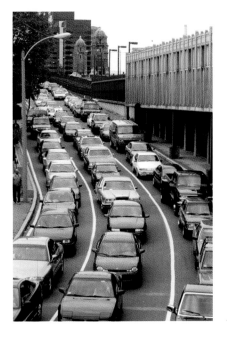

New laws in Massachusetts have been introduced to limit greenhouse-gas emissions from traffic.

" Unfortunately, much of current energy policy is driven by fears of global warming. It has led to undue emphasis on wind and solar power, on biofuels such as ethanol, and on schemes to sequester [capture] the CO_2 emitted from power plants. "

Science and Environmental Policy Project, 2006

Environmental politics

In the United States, some states are no longer waiting for the federal government to act, and instead are bringing in their own environmental laws. For example, California, Massachusetts, Oregon and Connecticut – among others – have all recently passed bills that will force industries to reduce their greenhouse-gas emissions and help to curb global warming. Such laws are often a response to the desires of the public to address ethical issues.

Not everyone is convinced that humans are destroying the environment, though – or that the Earth is under threat. Groups like the Heritage Foundation in the United States and the Scientific Alliance in the United Kingdom try to counterbalance the opinions coming from certain environmental pressure groups. However, these organisations are sometimes criticised for accepting large sums of money from businesses such as oil and mining companies, who have a vested interest in using the Earth's natural resources. This has raised the question of whether their opinions are ethical or driven by financial incentives.

YOU DECIDE

The Heritage Foundation is financially supported by a number of corporations, including Chevron Texaco, ExxonMobil and General Motors. Some of the findings made by the Heritage Foundation have influenced environmental policy in the United States.

? *Is it right for pressure groups to accept funding from corporations?*

? *Is there a danger that this kind of funding might bias the opinions of an organisation?*

? *Are any sources of funding truly unbiased?*

2 Power and Energy

Everything humans do needs energy – smiling, frowning, baking a cake, or sending an astronaut into space. The amount of energy that is powered by the Earth's natural resources has become a matter of increasing concern over the past few decades. Scientists are now trying to find ways of improving energy efficiency. One of the most important steps towards this is convincing people to change the way they use energy in their everyday lives.

Conservation of energy

Energy never disappears, it simply changes from one form to another. For example, the human body converts food into power, which is used for movement. A car burns petrol, converting the stored chemical energy into movement, heat and noise – all forms of energy.

In the case of a car, more than half of the energy from burning the fuel is turned into heat and sound. A car has low energy efficiency because so much of the energy is converted into a form that we cannot put to good use. Energy efficiency is a measure of how much useful energy a device produces. In general, cars have less than 50 per cent energy efficiency.

This map shows the energy consumption per capita across the world (in tonnes of oil equivalent). Canada uses the most energy per capita, while developing countries only account for 30 per cent of global total energy consumption.

> ❝ *An American uses six times as much energy, mostly fossil fuels, as the worldwide average, and 70 times more than a Bangladeshi. That same American consumes twice as much energy as do Western Europeans and three times as much as do Japanese.* ❞

Norman Myers and Jennifer Kent
Perverse Subsidies

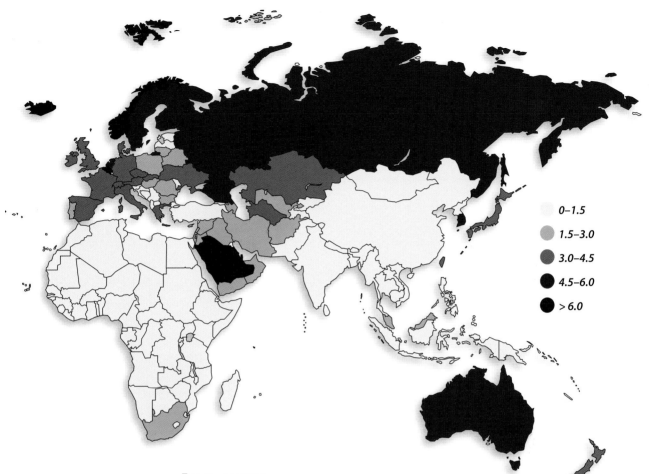

	0–1.5
	1.5–3.0
	3.0–4.5
	4.5–6.0
	> 6.0

Energy sources

The sources of the energy that we use fall into two groups: renewable and non-renewable. Renewable energy sources are those that can be replenished at the same rate they are used. These include wind, wave and solar power. Non-renewable energy sources are those that we use faster than we can replace them, such as coal, oil, gas and uranium.

To make life more convenient we sometimes make what are called 'secondary' sources of energy. These help us to store, move and deliver energy in an easy-to-use form. Electricity and hydrogen are examples of secondary energy sources. In most developed countries, houses, offices, shops and other buildings are connected to an electricity grid. This carries electricity from a power station along a system of cables to homes and workplaces.

TYPES OF ENERGY

There are two types of energy: kinetic and potential. Kinetic energy is the energy of motion. Anything that is moving has kinetic energy – electrons moving along a wire, molecules jiggling inside a crystal or light travelling from the Sun. Potential energy is energy that is stored, waiting to be converted into power, such as the water sitting behind a dam, molecular bonds inside a lump of coal, or the power inside a stretched rubber band.

Fossil fuels

Finding ways of harnessing and controlling different forms of energy has transformed our lives. In particular, fossil fuels (coal, oil and gas) have had a huge effect. These energy-rich substances were created millions of years ago, from the remains of plants and animals (fossils) that were heated and compressed inside the Earth. Today we use them to enable us to live in cold places, travel huge distances and communicate with people on the other side of the world. Fossil fuels supply 80 per cent of the world's energy needs, but they are diminishing fast – and once they are gone, they cannot be replaced. One of the greatest ethical dilemmas facing us all today is how to manage fossil-fuel consumption.

A convenient source of energy

The beauty of fossil fuels is their convenience. They are relatively easy to move around and the energy stays locked up inside them until we are ready to use it. For example, coal can

---

FOSSIL-FUEL CONSUMPTION

Fossil fuels have been mined all over the world for centuries. However, scientists are now estimating that reserves of these fuels are running very low. The most optimistic estimates predict that coal will last another 252 years, gas 72 years and oil just 32 years if they continue to be used at the rate they are now.

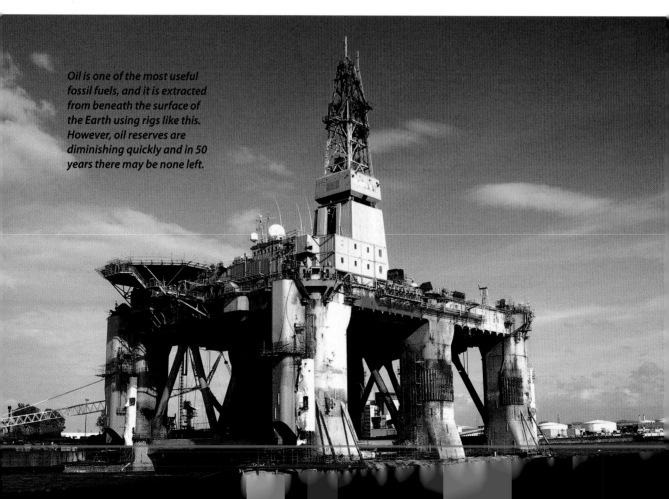

Oil is one of the most useful fossil fuels, and it is extracted from beneath the surface of the Earth using rigs like this. However, oil reserves are diminishing quickly and in 50 years there may be none left.

Mining for coal is a dirty, difficult and dangerous job. What is more, using coal for energy pumps out pollutants into the atmosphere.

be mined in Australia and then shipped to England to use to power a blast furnace to make steel. Meanwhile, gas can be piped all the way from its source to your door, powering the central heating in your home and keeping you warm.

But there are problems with fossil fuels, too. They are non-renewable and they release pollutants into the atmosphere, contributing to poor health and affecting the Earth's climate. Coal is particularly dirty and emits radioactive materials when it is burned.

Clean coal technology

Coal is one of the most polluting of all fossil fuels, but scientists have now developed a way of removing the impurities before it is burnt, making the coal burn more efficiently. Once it has been burnt, the smoke can be cleaned before it leaves the chimney, disposing of polluting gases like sulphur dioxide.

One of the latest technologies is 'carbon capture'. This involves collecting carbon dioxide from power plants before it can enter and damage the atmosphere and storing it deep underground, in places like disused mines. Locking up carbon dioxide in this way will help to combat global warming. However, capturing carbon dioxide uses significant amounts of energy. What is more, some scientists are now concerned that the carbon dioxide may leak from its underground store and end up polluting the atmosphere anyway.

YOU DECIDE

The Arctic National Wildlife Refuge lies in the north-west corner of Alaska. Many rare animal and bird species are found here, but the reserve is also valuable for its oil. There could be as much as 16 billion barrels of oil there – enough to power the United States for around two years. Extracting the oil may damage the environment.

? *In cases like this, should governments act in the best interests of people or the environment?*

? *Who does the oil belong to – the American people, the indigenous people who live on the refuge or everyone?*

Greenhouse gases

Carbon dioxide, water vapour and methane are all examples of greenhouse gases. In the atmosphere they hold on to heat and create a warm blanket of air around the Earth. Without them the Earth's surface would be around 30°C cooler and most life forms would not be able to survive.

Volcanoes are a natural source of greenhouse gases, pumping them out each time they erupt. Meanwhile, plants and trees are a natural sink for greenhouse gases, breathing them in when they photosynthesise, converting them into oxygen.

A rapid increase

Air samples that scientists have taken from bubbles inside ice cores show that the levels of carbon dioxide in the air have rocketed over the last 200 years. Before the Industrial Revolution – more than 200 years ago – carbon dioxide made up around 280 parts per million of air. By the year 2000 carbon dioxide made up 367 parts per million of air.

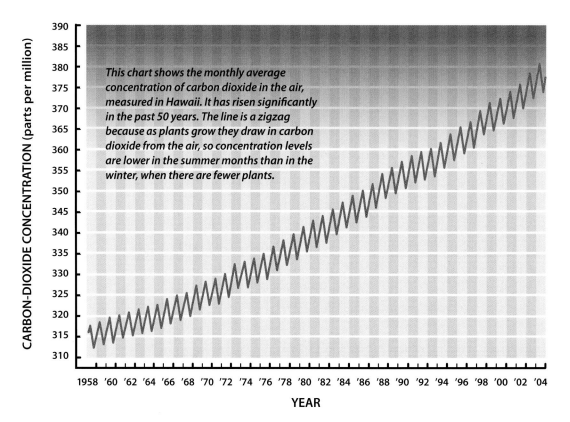

This chart shows the monthly average concentration of carbon dioxide in the air, measured in Hawaii. It has risen significantly in the past 50 years. The line is a zigzag because as plants grow they draw in carbon dioxide from the air, so concentration levels are lower in the summer months than in the winter, when there are fewer plants.

Burning fossil fuels for industry and clearing land (cutting down trees releases carbon dioxide) have caused much of this increase. Today we are producing twice as much carbon dioxide than trees and plants can convert back into oxygen. This imbalance is causing huge problems for the environment and is an area of great debate among scientists and policy-makers.

Warming up

This thicker blanket of greenhouse gases is causing the planet to heat up. Over the last 100 years the Earth's average surface temperature has risen by more than 0.5°C. Already this small change has had quite a dramatic effect. Global mean sea-level has increased by an average of more than 12 cm in the last century, Arctic sea ice has thinned by 40 per cent in recent decades, and the winter has shortened by between one and four days per decade over the last 40 years.

Climate scientists predict that by the year 2100 the global mean surface temperature will have increased by somewhere between 1.4 and 5.8°C. Extreme weather conditions such as floods, droughts and hurricanes are likely to become more commonplace, and further sea-level rises will swamp vast areas of land.

> **Because greenhouse gases continue to increase, we are, in effect, conducting a global climate experiment, neither planned nor controlled, the results of which may present unprecedented challenges to our wisdom and foresight as well as have significant impacts on our natural and societal systems.**

Statement issued by the American Meteorological Society, 2003

YOU DECIDE

The United States has not signed the Kyoto Protocol (see page 16), but individual states like California are taking the matter into their own hands, signing agreements to reduce greenhouse gases.

? *Who should take responsibility for reducing greenhouse gases – governments, states or individuals?*

? *Is it fair for wealthy developed nations to force developing countries like China and India to reduce their emissions?*

? *Are agreements like the Kyoto Protocol the best way to tackle global warming, or will new technologies provide an answer?*

Scientists predict that polar bears could become extinct by the end of the century, because their hunting grounds are being reduced as the sea ice thins and they are having to swim further to find food.

The Sizewell B nuclear power plant in the UK was built in the 1980s. Since then, there have been campaigns to have it shut down.

POWER FACTS

■ *A coal-fired power station releases more radioactivity into the environment than a nuclear power station.*

■ *One gram of uranium contains about the same amount of energy as three tonnes of coal.*

■ *A typical 1,000 megawatt nuclear power station (enough to power almost one million homes) produces around 30 tonnes (3 m³ when compressed) of high-level radioactive waste each year.*

A nuclear future?

Tackling global warming will probably mean significantly reducing the amount of fossil fuels we use. Although several alternatives are available, each of them raises a new set of ethical issues.

One potential substitute is nuclear energy. Nuclear energy is emitted when a neutron is absorbed into the nucleus of an atom and the atom splits into two lighter nuclei. This is known as nuclear fission and is the process that occurs inside nuclear power plants. The fuel used is the element uranium, which contains about three million times more energy than fossil fuels.

Around 17 per cent of the world's electricity is supplied by nuclear power plants. Unlike fossil fuels, no greenhouse gases are produced when making nuclear energy, although the mining of uranium does result in some greenhouse-gas emissions. Another advantage of nuclear power is that uranium is a common element, found in most rocks and soils.

However, nuclear power stations are very expensive to build and, after nuclear accidents like the Chernobyl disaster in Ukraine

In nuclear fission, a neutron is fired at the nucleus of an element like uranium. As the uranium nucleus splits, it produces energy in the form of heat. This is used to heat water, making steam, which in turn can power turbines.

Energy is produced

Neutron

Nucleus of uranium

Nucleus splits

YOU DECIDE

One of the main concerns about nuclear power is how to store the waste. Most radioactive waste needs to be stored for 10,000 years or more – equivalent to more than 300 human generations.

? *Is nuclear power fair on future generations – should they have to worry about our waste?*

? *Should every country have to dispose of its own nuclear waste, or is it acceptable to trade nuclear waste between countries?*

? *Do the risks associated with nuclear power outweigh the risks posed by global warming?*

in 1986, many people are concerned about the safety of nuclear power. Like fossil fuels, uranium will run out eventually. What is more, making nuclear power also produces radioactive waste, some of which needs to be stored for many thousands of years before it becomes safe. Some people are also concerned that if this waste gets into the wrong hands it could be used to make nuclear weapons.

Nuclear fusion

Another option is nuclear fusion – the energy produced when nuclei crash into each other and fuse together. This is the same process that fuels all stars, including our Sun, keeping them burning, and it is an attractive way of making energy on Earth. Nuclear fusion produces huge amounts of energy and there are no dangerous waste products or greenhouse gases.

However, it takes a lot of energy to get nuclear fusion started and, so far, no one has found a way of creating energy from nuclear fusion on Earth. An international team of scientists are working on the problem, and plans are underway to build an experimental reactor (ITER) at Cadarache in the south of France to research ways of making nuclear-fusion reactions.

3 Renewable Resources

Renewable energy sources are those that can be replenished as quickly as they are used. Wind, wave, solar, water and geothermal power are all examples. They are often seen as a solution to debates about global warming and the environment. But are renewable resources really the answer, and can they provide enough power for everyone in the world?

In general, renewable energy produces very little pollution and it is sustainable – resources can be replaced as fast as they are used. Most forms of renewable energy produce few greenhouse gases, making them very important in the fight against global warming. Groups campaigning for greener energy sources encourage the use of those that are renewable, such as wind and water power.

However, there are problems with renewable resources too – both practical and ethical. Generally they are not as efficient as fossil fuels or nuclear power, and large areas of

Capturing some kinds of renewable energy requires large areas of land, for example at solar farms like this in California.

The Dinorwig power station in Wales is a pumped storage hydroelectric scheme. Water is pumped to a reservoir at off-peak times and then released through turbines at peak times.

land have to be used to capture sufficient quantities of power. Also, many renewable energy technologies are expensive to build at the moment, although they might become cheaper if people start using them on a larger scale. A big ethical debate is therefore based around the monetary cost in relation to the cost to the environment.

Uneven distribution of energy

There is enough wind, sunshine and water to provide power for everyone in the world, but these resources are not always readily available where they are needed. For example, there is lots of solar energy – energy from the Sun – in the Sahara Desert, but very few people live there.

Perhaps the biggest problem of all is intermittency. Wind turbines only provide power when the wind blows, for example. Conventional fossil fuels and nuclear power stations can control their output and increase production when necessary. When renewable resources are being used, people have to rely on pumped storage hydroelectric schemes when there are surges in demand.

Decentralised power

Pumped storage could fill some of the gaps for renewable resources, but other solutions would also be needed. Currently scientists are investigating ways of storing renewable energy in special batteries.

However, if renewable resources are to be taken seriously, global power-distribution systems must change. Unlike fossil fuels and nuclear energy, renewable resources work much more efficiently when they operate on a small scale. Less energy is lost as it is converted into power, and every community makes the best use of the renewable resources available to it. Making this kind of change in infrastructure would be expensive.

YOU DECIDE

Renewable power sources are not as efficient as fossil fuels or nuclear power, and at the moment they are more expensive to produce.

? *Should we be willing to accept these costs because of the long-term benefits of halting global warming?*

? *Would it be better to wait for more efficient renewable technologies to be developed, rather than facing the issues caused by wind turbines or solar panels?*

Wind farms like this in Germany can provide clean energy from a renewable resource – but they also cause noise pollution, use up large tracts of land and, some argue, are an unsightly addition to the landscape.

WIND FARMS

Although the United States has several important wind farms, currently less than one per cent of electricity there is sourced from wind power, whereas in Denmark around 20 per cent of electricity consumption is covered by electricity produced at wind farms. Wind turbines could provide 20 per cent of America's electricity, by covering just one per cent of land with wind farms.

Wind energy

Antarctica is probably the windiest place in the world, but there is no need to go all the way to Antarctica to feel a breeze – wind is everywhere. Traditionally people have captured the wind's energy using windmills and used it to grind grain, pump water and even saw wood. So can wind provide us with energy today?

Wind turbines gather energy from the wind and convert it into electricity. The three blades of the turbine are pushed around by the wind. This spins a shaft, which connects to a generator and makes electricity.

A clean solution

The big advantage of wind energy is that it produces no greenhouse gases. There is also no air pollution or waste products, and once the turbine has been constructed, the energy source is free. Germany is currently the world's leading wind-power nation, followed by Spain and the United States.

Places with strong, steady winds are best for wind turbines. Unfortunately, these windy places are often wilderness areas, which provide an important habitat for animals, birds and plants. Some people are concerned that wind turbines could have a negative impact on the wildlife in these special environments. Others say that wind turbines are unsightly and spoil the countryside.

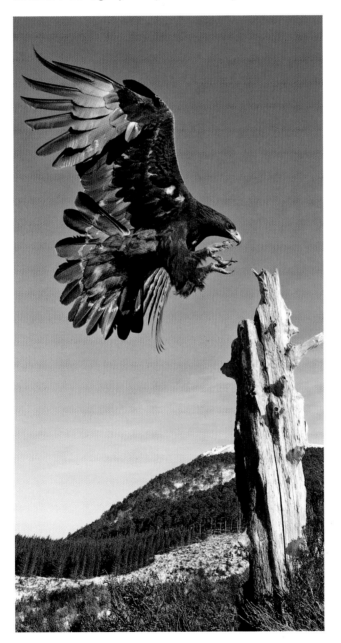

Harming nature

In particular, the turbines can present a threat to birds and bats, especially if a wind farm is situated on a bird migratory route. Plants and animals can also suffer during the construction phase, when new roads are built to transport the turbine to its site, and large amounts of concrete are used to support the turbine. Some of these environmental impacts can be avoided by erecting the wind farms out at sea, but this is more costly. Are these small prices to pay for the human and environmental benefits of wind energy?

The construction of wind farms in places where rare birds like the golden eagle are still found is causing concern among some groups of people, who fear that the destruction of the birds' habitats may result in them dying out altogether.

66 *Wind farms must be located away from narrow bird migration routes and important feeding, breeding and roosting areas. They must not be permitted where they would have adverse impacts on nationally and internationally protected wildlife sites.* 99

Royal Society for the Protection of Birds

Water power

Water is one of the most powerful forces of nature, and scientists are now looking at water power as a possible alternative to energy from non-renewable resources. Crashing waves, tidal cycles, gushing rivers and reservoirs are all full of energy. High-level lakes contain a lot of potential (stored) energy. Hydroelectric power stations are one way of capturing this energy, by releasing a controlled flow of water from an upper reservoir to a lower one. The water turns a turbine on the way.

Mountains and rain

Countries like China, Canada, Austria, Norway and Scotland, which have plenty of rainfall, mountains and valleys, are ideal places for hydroelectric schemes. It is a relatively cheap source of energy and it is renewable. In addition, hydroelectric power overcomes the intermittency problem by storing water when it rains and slowly releasing the energy as it is needed.

Most of the best sites for hydroelectric power schemes have already been used in developed nations, but in developing countries there is scope for building more large-scale schemes. The ethical questions about the use of water power surround the damage that can be caused to the environment by the construction of such plants. Blocking a river with a large concrete dam provides a barrier to fish and causes silt to build up. Many animals, plants and people can also lose their homes when a valley is flooded.

The Jochenstein hydroelectric power station lies on the River Danube between Austria and Germany. Countries like these are well-suited to hydroelectric schemes because they have relatively high levels of rainfall.

HYDROELECTRICITY

■ *Around 20 per cent of the world's electricity is generated by hydroelectric power.*

■ *In 1975, a typhoon caused 62 dams in China's Henan Province to fail. An estimated 26,000 people died from the flooding and nearly six million buildings collapsed.*

■ *If 0.1 per cent of the energy of the oceans was converted to electricity, it would be enough to supply the world's energy demand more than five times over.*

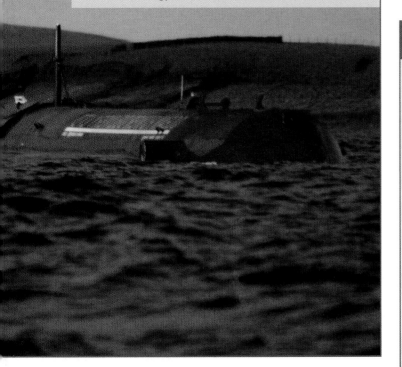

The Pelamis Wave Energy Converter has been used in a 'wave farm' constructed in 2006 off the coast of Portugal. It converts the energy of surface waves on the ocean into electricity.

Waves and tides

Gathering energy from the ocean is another option. The push and pull of the Moon sucks the oceans in and out twice a day, moving vast amounts of water. This movement creates energy. The challenge is working out how to capture these forms of energy. Scientists and engineers are working hard to solve this problem and there are now several wave and tidal plants in operation in countries like France and Canada. Japan also has a programme that is finding ways of harnessing wave energy to provide power to coastal communities. However, at the moment the cost of building tidal plants is preventing large-scale development.

YOU DECIDE

When it is finished in 2009 the Three Gorges Dam in China will be the largest in the world. More than one million people have already been displaced by the building of the dam, and many archeological and cultural sites will be flooded. It will supply less than three per cent of China's electricity needs.

? *How should the displaced people be compensated for their loss of housing and land, and who should pay for this?*

? *Is it safe to build such a large dam, especially in a country that suffers from earthquakes? Would you live downstream of this dam?*

? *Is it fair of developed nations to criticise this dam, when they have already benefited from building large hydroelectric schemes?*

Solar power

Solar power is one of the most abundant sources of renewable
energy. At the Equator the Sun provides around 1,000 watts of
energy per square metre – equivalent to about 10 light-bulbs'
worth of power. However, the debates surrounding the use of
solar energy are similar to those of other renewable resources.
In order to capture enough energy to make it viable, large
areas of land need to be used, with possible consequences
of damaging natural habitats and displacing people.

Solar-energy factories

There are several ways of gathering solar energy. Solar panels
on the roofs of buildings focus the Sun's rays and use them to
heat water in pipes underneath. Photovoltaic cells are similar,
but these special cells have a more sophisticated technology
that turns the Sun's heat into an electric current, which can be
used to power the home.

Solar energy can also be captured on a larger scale. The
largest solar plant in the world is in the Mojave Desert at
Kramer Junction, California. Its banks of curving, shiny mirrors
concentrate sunlight and heat a fluid, which is used to make
steam to turn a turbine and generate electricity.

In Australia there are
plans to build a 1-km high
'solar tower'. The Sun's
warmth will heat air,
which then rises through
the tower and spins
turbines, creating power.

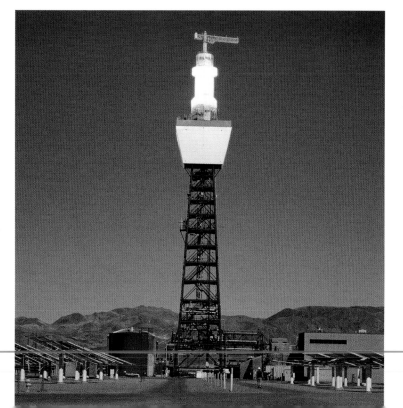

*This solar power tower is
at the Barstow plant in
California. Mirrors at the
bottom of the tower focus the
Sun's rays on to a receiver at
the top, which creates steam
from the heat. The steam is
used to power turbines,
generating electricity.*

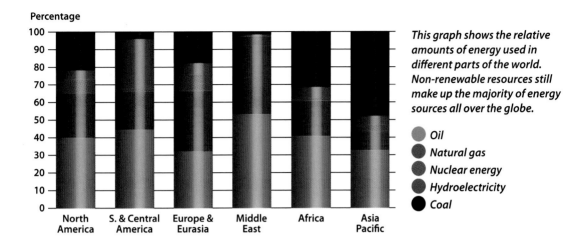

Percentage

This graph shows the relative amounts of energy used in different parts of the world. Non-renewable resources still make up the majority of energy sources all over the globe.

● *Oil*
● *Natural gas*
● *Nuclear energy*
● *Hydroelectricity*
● *Coal*

Down below

Heat can also come from deep underground. The temperature at the centre of the Earth is around 5,500°C – about the same as it is on the surface of the Sun. Volcanic countries, such as Iceland, have a superhighway to this heat source and can tap into it by piping up the water from hot springs. This can be used directly to heat houses, or indirectly – using steam to drive a turbine and make electricity.

Non-volcanic countries can also make use of the Earth's heat. Although not as hot as the volcanic areas, the upper three metres of the Earth's surface have a constant temperature of around 10–16°C. Special heat pumps absorb the heat from below by piping water down to around 20 m and then pumping it back up again. For every unit of electricity used to pump the heat, three to four units of heat are produced. When renewable energy powers the pump it offers a truly green solution.

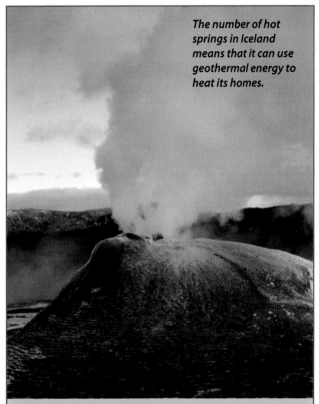

The number of hot springs in Iceland means that it can use geothermal energy to heat its homes.

GEOTHERMAL ENERGY

In Reykjavik, Iceland, more than 95 per cent of the buildings are heated with geothermal water pumped from deep wells. Although geothermal energy is an environmentally friendly solution, it is not suitable everywhere because installing the system involves disrupting building foundations and surrounding land.

4 Transport and Travel

The world has opened up dramatically over the past few decades. Now, thanks to cars, boats, aeroplanes, trains and buses, we can travel further, more frequently, and in greater comfort than ever before. This globalisation in transport and travel has given rise to several serious ethical questions about the effects it is having on natural resources and the environment.

In large cities like Los Angeles, a permanent smog hangs in the air from pollution caused by traffic emissions.

Many countries are now encouraging people to cycle rather than use cars by creating special cycle lanes along the roads.

Transport pollution

Almost all the forms of transport we use are powered by fossil fuels, especially oil. Vehicles need an energy source that is stable (not explosive or flammable), portable, lightweight, high-energy and that can be turned on or off at will. Petroleum is ideal. It is relatively stable, easily transportable, packed full of energy and easy to stop and start. This convenience comes at a cost, though. Burning oil in engines produces greenhouse gases as well as a cocktail of other chemicals that are damaging to health. Carbon monoxide, nitrogen monoxide, benzene, lead and tiny particles are just some of the things that can result in health problems.

Much of modern life depends on transport – and not just for holidays. Food, clothes and almost everything else people use rely on some form of transport to get them into the shops. In developed countries nearly 40 per cent of energy consumption is due to transport.

A growing problem

The issues surrounding the use of natural resources in travel and transport are causing increasing alarm in many countries. For example, in 2005 people in the United Kingdom covered a staggering 797 billion passenger kilometres – equivalent to 13,350 km per person. Ninety-two per cent of that travelling was by road, six per cent by rail and 1.2 per cent by air. Compare this to 1951, when people in the UK covered just 218 billion passenger kilometres (4,343 km per person), with 82 per cent by road, 18 per cent by rail and only 0.1 per cent by air.

Travelling has become faster and more affordable, tempting us all to travel more. Whether it is holidays in exotic foreign locations, commuting longer distances to work, or simply driving to the shops instead of walking, we are often on the move. Just because it is easier and more convenient to use transport, though, should we be ignoring the effect it is having on the environment?

YOU DECIDE

Travelling by car, boat, plane or train produces greenhouse-gas emissions and other pollutants that are bad for health and the environment.

? *Do we need to travel as much as we do?*

? *Would you consider travelling less, or using less-polluting transport (for example a bicycle instead of a car) for the sake of the environment?*

? *Should the government discourage people from travelling by taxing transport more heavily?*

Air travel

Some forms of transport are more polluting than others and this is an area in which every individual can make ethical decisions that will affect the Earth's future.

For example, flying might be a convenient and fast way of getting around, but it is one of the most environmentally damaging methods of transport. Aircraft have a greater impact on climate change than ground-based transport. The water vapour that comes out of an aircraft exhaust creates clouds (contrails), which intercept sunlight and change the temperature of the atmosphere. Add to this the 700 million tonnes of carbon dioxide emitted by commercial aircraft every year and you have a recipe for global warming.

Aircraft can also cause problems at ground level. Take-off and landing can cause noise pollution, and usually acres of countryside are lost to make way for tarmac runways.

Studies over the past 10 years have shown that aircraft contrails are likely to be a contributing factor to global warming.

> **"** *Increased cirrus [cloud] coverage, attributable to air traffic, could account for nearly all of the warming observed over the United States for nearly 20 years… Human activity has a visible and significant impact on cloud cover and, therefore, on climate. It indicates that contrails should be included in climate change scenarios.* **"**

Patrick Minnis
Scientist, NASA's Langley Research Center

CARBON NEUTRALITY

In some countries, including Holland and the United Kingdom, programmes have been introduced to help individuals gain 'carbon credits'. Each time you take a flight you donate money to an organisation such as Trees for Life or Trees for Travel. This money is used to plant trees, which absorb carbon dioxide. This is a way of helping neutralise the effects of pollution caused by air travel.

SUVs emit significantly more carbon dioxide than ordinary cars. Some pressure groups are campaigning to ban the use of SUVs in towns and cities.

Personal cars

In most developed countries a high percentage of the population owns a private car. A car gives us the freedom to move around wherever and whenever we want, and to carry passengers and goods from one place to another. Like aircraft, though, personal cars are heavy contributors to global warming and atmospheric pollution.

The average car produces around four tonnes of carbon dioxide each year. Drive a gas-guzzling SUV and this can easily triple to around 12 tonnes of carbon dioxide per year. What is more, in busy cities like Los Angeles, vehicle emissions can create a toxic smog that is bad for people's health and the environment.

Public transport

Travelling on a public train, bus or boat tends to be less damaging to the environment because the journey (and resulting emissions) are shared between many people. On average, using public transport can reduce your emissions by two-thirds or more compared to travelling in a car. However, in many countries the systems of public transport are not widespread, reliable or cheap enough to convince people to use them instead of their private cars.

YOU DECIDE

Although air travel is the quickest way of travelling, it is extremely damaging to the environment. It might take longer to travel by boat, for example, but such methods cause far less pollution.

? *Would you consider alternative methods of transport when you go on holiday?*

? *Should airlines have to pay a tax on their fuel?*

? *How could such a tax be implemented globally?*

31

The growing market for palm oil as a biofuel is encouraging Indonesians to fell tropical forest, reducing the habitat for endangered species like the orang-utan.

Biofuels

Several ethical alternatives to polluting fuels are being developed. Filling a car tank with turkey guts might sound unpleasant, but it could be a 'green' alternative to oil. A biofuel is any fuel from a recently living organism (like a tree) or its by-product (like turkey guts or manure from cows). These are renewable and could help to reduce greenhouse gases. Compared to fossil fuels, which locked up carbon from millions of years ago, plants and trees captured their carbon more recently, so burning them does not result in an overall increase of carbon dioxide in the atmosphere.

Many plants can be used to produce 'bioethanol' and 'biodiesel', alternatives to petrol and diesel for road transport. Ordinary cars can run on a blend of five per cent biofuel and 95 per cent petrol. Meanwhile, making a few changes to the engine enables vehicles to be run on pure vegetable oil.

Converting cars to run on biofuel would be relatively painless and easy to do. However, growing biofuels can be damaging for the environment, especially if tropical forests are cut down to make space for biofuel fields. Moreover, biofuel still contributes to air pollution and it cannot yet be used in aircraft.

YOU DECIDE

One possible way of encouraging people to travel less would be to introduce a 'carbon credits' scheme. Each time you fill the car with petrol, take a flight, or even turn the heating up a notch at home, you would use up some of your carbon quota. At the end of the year those people who have a surplus of carbon credits could sell them to those people who have run out.

? *Is it fair to ration carbon in this way?*

? *Should everyone be given the same carbon quota or should some people be allowed more, for example someone who lives in a very cold country?*

Hydrogen

Another possible solution to the transport problem is hydrogen. This can be burned, like oil, or reacted with oxygen inside a 'fuel cell' to produce electricity. However, unlike fossil and nuclear fuels, hydrogen cannot be mined; it has to be made. It can be produced from hydrocarbons such as methane, or extracted from water using electrolysis, a process that uses a lot of energy. With a few rather expensive exceptions (like wind- or water-powered electrolysis) these procedures produce greenhouse gases.

Even if it was possible to find a cheap and clean way of producing hydrogen, it would be costly and difficult to convert everyone's cars and homes to run on hydrogen. Is this really a viable option?

Hydrogen fuel-cell cars are very clean, emitting only heat and water from their exhausts. They are also more efficient – offering two to three times higher mileage on equivalent energy. It is possible to buy hydrogen cars now, but they are very expensive.

5 Wood and Water

Energy is not the only natural resource that humans use in large quantities. Water, timber, rocks and minerals are all vital too. For example, most people live in houses made of stone, brick or wood. Every day we drink and wash with water. Overuse of these resources can threaten the environment.

Nearly three-quarters of the world is covered in water, but almost all of it is salty. Only three per cent of the water on Earth is fresh. Two thirds of this is locked up in ice-caps and glaciers. Water is probably the most precious resource on Earth and yet most people are very wasteful about how they use it. The average American uses around 380 litres of water every day – more than enough to make a bath overflow. Most of this water is flushed down the toilet, sprinkled on the garden or used to wash the car.

The processes of evaporation and rainfall keep water on the move around the world. However, the distribution of freshwater around the globe is not evenly balanced.

Where does water come from?

Some of our water comes from reservoirs and lakes, which are replenished by rainfall. The remainder is usually groundwater, which has trickled through cracks in the Earth and is pumped up from deep underground. Some groundwater has been lying beneath the surface of the Earth for thousands of year.

Water is moved around the Earth by the processes of evaporation and rainfall. However, the rain does not fall evenly, and some places get much more than they need while others remain parched. As the world's population grows and lifestyles in many countries improve, water consumption increases. Sometimes there just isn't enough water to go around.

Water storage in the atmosphere

Water storage in ice and snow

Condensation

Precipitation

Snowmelt

Streamflow

Evaporation

Infiltration

Freshwater storage

Spring

Surface runoff

Water storage in oceans

Groundwater discharge

Groundwater storage

Today, rusting fishing boats lie scattered on dry land in what was once the Aral Sea, and the seashore is over 100 km away.

The disappearing sea

Aralsk, a small city in south-western Kazakhstan, used to be a thriving fishing port, sitting on the banks of the Aral Sea in central Asia. During the last 50 years the sea has shrunk to less than half its original area. The water that is left is very salty and most of the fish have died. People living in the area suffer from lack of fresh water and health problems due to the toxic dust that blows up from what was once the seabed. Water that would have once gushed into the Aral Sea is now diverted to irrigate crops like rice, melon, cereals and cotton in Kazakhstan and Uzbekistan.

Conflict over water use is likely to become worse in the future. Climate changes are predicted to bring more extreme weather such as floods and droughts. A recent World Water Development Report estimated that by 2050 at least one in four people is likely to live in a country affected by chronic freshwater shortage.

WATER USAGE
Irrigation accounts for around 70 per cent of global water usage. Industry uses up a further 15 per cent, while the remaining 15 per cent goes on household use.

YOU DECIDE

Producing a kilo of bananas requires 400 litres of water. A kilo of tomatoes needs just 40 litres. Over the last 40 years the River Jordan has been reduced to a trickle as farmers in Israel, Syria, Jordan and Palestine divert the water to irrigate tropical crops like bananas, mangoes and avocados.

? *Should people be allowed to grow water-thirsty crops in countries like Israel, where there is not enough rain and they rely on irrigation?*

? *How can – and should – other countries intervene?*

? *Would you buy a banana that had been grown in the Israeli desert?*

Trees and the environment

For thousands of years humans have been building things from wood. Even today, with many new materials available, wood products can still be seen everywhere – books, magazines, tables, doors, even whole buildings. Wood might be extremely useful to humans, but the trees from which wood comes also play an important part in environmental balance. Trees and plants take in carbon dioxide from the atmosphere and give out oxygen, providing us with fresh air to breathe. In addition, they help to keep the air clean by absorbing some of the pollutants from power stations, industry and cars. The rate at which trees are being cut down is now a matter of grave concern to environmentalists.

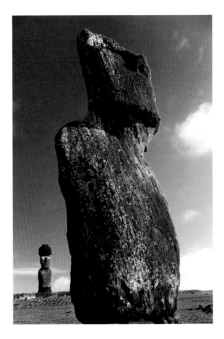

Some archeologists think that the Easter Islanders deforested their island between AD 1200 and 1500 in order to erect statues like this one.

YOU DECIDE

The island of Tasmania is home to some of the world's tallest and oldest trees, but these are rapidly disappearing as the trees are felled. Logging is an important industry in Tasmania, providing more than 7,000 people with jobs.

? *Should other countries be preventing Tasmania from cutting down its trees?*

? *Do we have a right to stop people from doing what they want with their natural resources?*

? *Is there a way that Tasmania could keep its trees without adversely affecting local people and economies?*

Clearing the land

Easter Island is a remote island in the Pacific Ocean, which has been inhabited for around 1,500 years. Around 500 years ago the people suffered a catastrophe when they ran out of trees. They could no longer make boats to go fishing and the deforestation led to soil erosion, making it difficult to grow crops. The few people that survived are thought to have resorted to cannibalism.

The problem of deforestation has grown dramatically in recent years. Currently we are cutting down trees faster than we can replace them. When these trees are cut down or burned they release carbon back into the atmosphere and contribute to global warming.

One reason for deforestation is to make space for farmland. In the Amazon rainforest in Brazil, farmers have cleared the trees in order to grow soybeans and rear cattle. Brazil is now the world's biggest exporter of beef and the ranchers are growing rich. In the process, however, native people have lost their homes and livelihoods, plants and animals have become extinct, and global temperatures have continued to rise. Already nearly one-fifth of Brazil's rainforest has disappeared.

17 June 2002

28 June 2006

These satellite images show how much
of Brazil's rainforest has been cleared in
the space of just four years. If clearance
continues at this rate, scientists estimate
that the Amazon rainforest will have
disappeared by 2050.

The map on the right shows the difference in
deforested areas between 2002 and 2006.
The largest cleared areas are red, areas that
had no forest in 2002 are white and areas
that were still forested in 2006 are grey.

6 The Environment and You

The way we choose to live our lives can have a huge impact on the environment and its resources. Below are some examples of the different lifestyles people enjoy, and the ways in which our actions affect the environment every day.

Joe

Joe Planter is 15 years old and lives in San Francisco with his mum, dad, sister Kim and dog Dudley. When he is not at school Joe likes to go skateboarding and mountain biking with his friends and listens to music on his iPod. He also supports his local basketball team – the Golden State Warriors – watching matches at home on the family's giant plasma-screen TV.

Joe and Kim catch the bus to school each day, taking a packed lunch made by Mrs Planter. The Planters are all vegetarian, but Joe sometimes has a sneaky burger when he is out with his friends. When Joe gets home from school he walks Dudley, usually in Golden Gate Park. At weekends the family loads up the car, an SUV, with bikes and heads off to Marin County for a ride. Every winter the family goes skiing for a week in Yosemite National Park. In summer they tend to take a beach holiday on the Californian coast.

Driving an SUV can cause much more damage to the environment than driving an ordinary car.

> 66 *The ultimate test of man's conscience may be his willingness to sacrifice something today for future generations whose words of thanks will not be heard.* 99

Gaylord Nelson
Co-founder of Earth Day

Fieke

Fieke Van Rijn is 14 years old and lives with her mum, dad and two sisters on a cheese farm near the town of Uithoorn in the Netherlands. Each day the girls get a lift to school in Mr Van Rijn's cheese van, after which he delivers his cheeses to the shops. In her spare time Fieke likes to ride horses and sometimes enters competitions on her pony, Nassau.

As well as eating the cheese made on their farm, the Van Rijns grow their own vegetables and buy their meat from the local butcher. At weekends the Van Rijns usually relax at home, or load the horses into their horse wagon and drive to an event. Every summer Mr Van Rijn's brother comes to look after the farm and the family have a two-week holiday. Last year they went on safari in Kenya. This year they are going to climb Mount Fuji in Japan.

YOU DECIDE

Joe and Fieke lead very different lifestyles, but which is better?

? *What kind of impact do they each have on the environment, who uses the most resources and who creates the most pollution?*

? *Joe and his family eat a lot of soya (grown in the Amazon) and buy imported fruit and vegetables. Fieke's family eats home-grown vegetables and locally sourced meat. What kind of impact do these different diets have on the environment? Can being vegetarian help to save resources and energy?*

? *What kind of changes could Joe and Fieke make to their lives to reduce their greenhouse-gas emissions from travel?*

Buying food from a local farm, or even making or growing it yourself, has many environmental advantages over shopping at the supermarket.

Old versus new

It is not just governments and scientists who need to address the ethical questions surrounding the use of natural resources and the environment. These are issues that everyone can act on. What kind of impact do you, your family and your friends have on the environment? Could you change your lifestyle and use up fewer natural resources?

How old is your refrigerator-freezer at home? If it is more than 10 years old then it probably uses up much more electricity than a modern model. Would it be better to replace it with a new one? Elderly refrigerators sometimes consume more than three times as much energy as new, energy-efficient models. But keeping your food cool is only half the picture. What about the energy it took to source the raw materials and build the refrigerator before it reached your home?

When replacing old goods, like cars, refrigerators, washing machines, computers and mobile phones, it is important to consider the whole life cycle of the object – from cradle to grave – and to ensure that the old goods are recycled wherever possible.

Recycling is one of the main ways in which individuals can help save energy. In this recycling plant in Germany, electrical goods from mobile phones to freezers can be recycled.

Organic versus local

Growing plants organically means that chemical fertilisers, pesticides and herbicides are not used, and the farming tends to be less mechanised. Generally this is good for wildlife and encourages a greater diversity of species. However, the yield from an organic farm is usually less, meaning that more land would need to be farmed if everyone in the world ate organic food.

Another consideration is how far the food has travelled to reach your plate. Is it better to buy organic green beans from Kenya or non-organic green beans from a farm just down the road?

Non-organic farming gives higher yields, but can be detrimental to plants and wildlife.

Turn out the light

Sometimes very small changes can make a big difference if everyone does them. Leaving televisions and other gadgets on standby wastes huge amounts of energy. Meanwhile, taking a bath instead of a shower can use up to five times as much water. This is one area in which the dilemmas can also be resolved with the help of every individual.

If you live in Scotland is it better to buy local tomatoes that have been grown in heated greenhouses, or imported Spanish tomatoes that grew under the Sun?

YOU DECIDE

Making small changes in everyday habits could have a big effect on resources and the environment if everyone took responsibility.

? *Is it right to impose changes such as car sharing, compulsory recycling and water restrictions (hose-pipe bans during drought for example)?*

? *Can voluntary individual action made a significant difference, or should we wait until governments force us to change our ways?*

Timeline

1962
Rachel Carson publishes *Silent Spring*.

1969
Friends of the Earth is founded.

1970
The first Earth Day is held, and millions of people all over the world demonstrate in favour of cleaning up the environment.

1979
The Three Mile Island nuclear power plant in the United States partially melts down. James Lovelock published the Gaia theory.

1982
The World Resources Institute is founded in the United States to find ways of managing global resources without compromising human needs.

1986
Explosions at the nuclear power plant in Chernobyl, Ukraine, create the world's worst nuclear power accident. Thirty-one people die immediately and 200 become seriously ill shortly afterwards from the effects of the radiation. Eight years after the incident experts estimate that more than 8,000 people have died from diseases caused by the radiation.

1989
The oil tanker *Exxon Valdez* runs aground in Alaska, spilling millions of gallons of oil, threatening wildlife.

1991
The United Nations Antarctic Treaty comes into force, banning mining and limiting pollution in the Antarctic region.

1992
The Earth Summit is held in Brazil, focusing on helping developing countries find ways of adopting environmentally friendly processes, and discussing issues such as rates of deforestation and climate change.

2000
The European Union bans the used of leaded petrol.

2002
The German government announces that it plans to increase its wind generation over the next 25 years. The World Summit on Sustainable Development is held in South Africa.

2005
The Kyoto Protocol comes into force – those who have ratified the agreement have committed to reducing carbon emissions in their countries.

2006
Greenpeace activists try to prevent the unloading of a coal shipment in Thailand.

2007
Construction begins on the experimental reactor (ITER) at Cadarache in the south of France to research ways of making nuclear-fusion reactions.

Further Information

● Books

Climate Change Begins at Home: Life on the Two-way street of Global Warming
by Dave Reay, Palgrave Macmillan, 2006

Save Energy, Save the Planet by Claire Llewellyn, Chrysalis Books, 2005

Silent Spring by Rachel Carson, Penguin Books, 2000

Sustainable Development by Clive Gifford, Heinemann Library, 2004

Sustainable Futures series by various authors, Evans Brothers, 2006

The Ages of Gaia by James Lovelock, Oxford University Press, 2000

The Earth's Resources by Richard and Louise Spilsbury, Evans Brothers, 2006

New Technology Series by various authors, Evans Brothers, 2008

● Websites

www.greenpeace.org/international/ Greenpeace.

www.earthday.net/default.aspx Earth Day Network.

www.foei.org/ Friends of the Earth.

www.heritage.org/ The Heritage Foundation.

www.aim.org/ Accuracy in Media.

www.sepp.org/ Science and Environmental Policy Project.

www.eia.doe.gov/ Energy Information Administration.

www.coolkidsforacoolclimate.com/Take%20Action/TakeActionIndex.htm
Cool Kids for a Cool Climate

http://news.bbc.co.uk/1/hi/in_depth/sci_tech/2004/climate_change/default.stm
BBC climate change 'In Depth'.

www.awea.org/ American Wind Energy Association.

www.nrel.gov/wind/ National Wind Technology Center.

www.chooseclimate.org/ Choose Climate – a website to calculate your own transport emissions.

www.changingworldtech.com/ Changing World Technologies (the company that converts turkey waste into fuel).

www.ran.org/ Rainforest Action Network.

www.carbontrust.co.uk/default.ct The Carbon Trust.

Glossary

biofuel fuel that is made from a recently living organism or its by-products.

civilisation advanced human society where people live in cities and get their food from agriculture.

contrail artificial cloud produced by the condensation trail from the exhaust of an aircraft engine.

deforestation cutting down trees and converting forested areas to non-forested areas.

electrolysis method of breaking the bonds in elements and compounds by passing an electric current through them.

ethics a formalised set of rules generally developed from widely held morals. Ethical codes may become accepted by a whole society, when they often develop into laws (see *morals*).

evaporation process where atoms or molecules gain energy and change from being in a liquid state to a gaseous state.

fossil fuel fuel formed in the past from the remains of animals and plants (fossils).

Gaia theory named after a Greek goddess, Gaia theory was proposed by British scientist James Lovelock and suggests that the Earth behaves as if it were a living organism.

globalisation operating on a global scale.

global warming gradual rise in temperature of the Earth's atmosphere caused by the burning of fossil fuels.

greenhouse gas atmospheric gas that absorbs infrared radiation from the Sun and helps to keep the Earth warm.

groundwater water located beneath the ground, in cracks, pores and fractures within soil or rocks.

hydroelectric energy energy captured from moving water.

incineration burning of solid waste material.

Industrial Revolution major change in technological, economic and social conditions that began in the late eighteenth century in Britain and spread throughout the world.

intermittent not continuous.

irrigation supplying water to crops and plants to supplement or replace rainfall water.

kinetic energy energy arising from movement.

Kyoto Protocol agreement made under the United Nations Framework Convention on Climate Change (UNFCCC), which commits